LOTS OF FUN TO PAINT

Published by the William Collins + World Publishing Co., Inc.
2080 West 117th Street, Cleveland, Ohio 44111
First American Printing 1974
ISBN 0-529-05067-6 (Trade Edition)
ISBN 0-529-05068-4 (Library Edition)
Library of Congress Catalog Card Number 72-13397
© 1971 Editions Fernand Nathan
Printed in the United States of America

Colette Lamarque

LOTS OF FUN TO PAINT

COLLINS WORLD

COLOR CONTRASTS

Bright shapes on a black background . . .

Cover a sheet of white paper completely with streaks of bright color — use felt pens, colored inks or poster paints.

When the paper is dry, draw some very simple shapes on it (or draw the same shape a few times). You will find it easier if you use tracing paper for this. With a fine brush and black paint, carefully paint around the shapes you have drawn, and go on to fill in the whole background.

To trace: Put tracing paper over the drawing you want to use and copy over the outline. Place the tracing paper over your brightly colored sheet of paper and go over the outline with a well-sharpened pencil. This makes a dented line on the colored paper.

Another way to make bright shapes: Place an object (try an autumn leaf) on your brightly colored sheet. Draw around this with a pencil and carefully paint everything outside the outline with black paint or India ink.

EXOTIC FLOWERS

1. To make short, squarish petals, use a brush with short, hard bristles and very thick paint (from a tube or very thick poster paint).

    Make a center and, with your brush well loaded with paint, put petals all around it.

2. For these longer petals, use a brush with soft bristles and paint which you have thinned with water. Put the tip of the brush on to the paper and then lay it down to make the long petals.

3. With a fine brush, take a blob of very thick paint and put it straight on to the paper to form a thick dot.

4. Sharpen the end of a used wooden match. Dip it in thick paint and draw the stems with it.

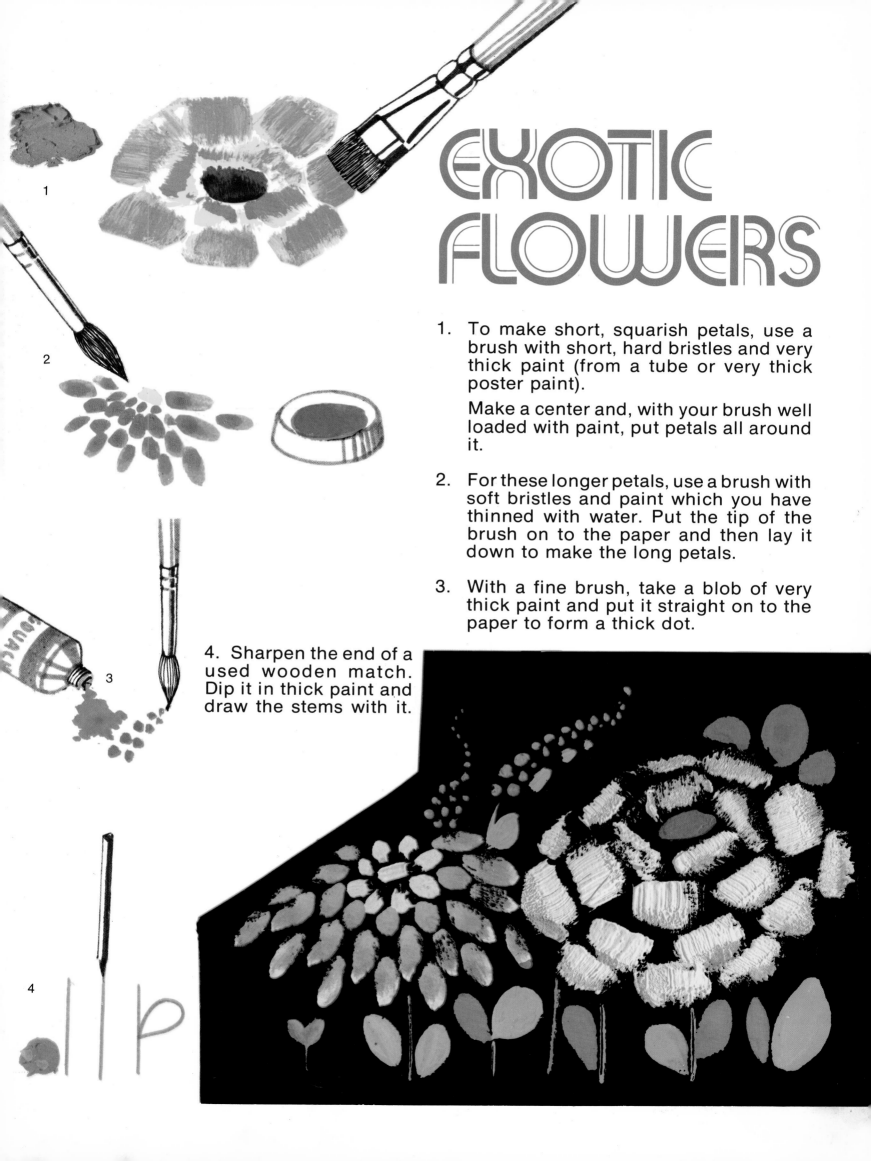

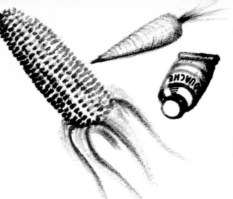

VEGETABLE PRINTING

A BASKET OF CHERRIES

A sheet of paper,
an ear of corn,
a carrot,
some thick poster paint.

THE BASKET

Cut the ends off the ear of corn (1).
Coat it in thick paint. With the palm of your hand, roll it on a sheet of paper (2).
(It may be necessary to do this more than once.)

THE CHERRIES

Cut the end off a carrot (3).
Coat the cut end in red paint, and use it as a printing stick to make the cherries (4).

THE LEAVES

Split the carrot you used for the cherries to make a printing stick of a half-circle. With this, and green paint, you can print the leaves.
. . . Use a sharpened used wooden match to paint in the stems.

By loading your printing sticks with more or less paint, you can make darker or lighter cherries and leaves.

MAKE A POTATO PICTURE

1. Cut a large potato into sticks.
2. Dip the end of a stick into thick poster paint.
3. This is your potato printing stick!

Try printing different colors on top of each other.

Sticks of different sizes and shapes can be used.

THE CASTLE

The walls: Draw an outline in pencil.
Cover the surfaces with a potato printing stick dipped in thick paint (1,2,3).

The roof: Cut a potato stick to make a triangular printing shape. (Other vegetables, radishes or carrots for example, can be used.)

Use your imagination to put the finishing touches on the picture.

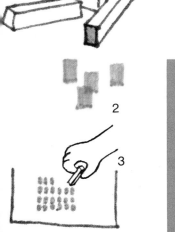

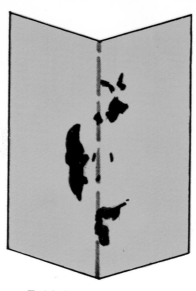

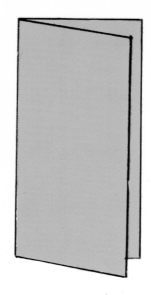

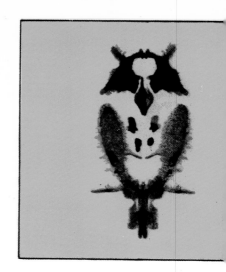

On a sheet of fine paper, make some blots with ink or paint.

Fold the paper in half, with the blots to the inside.

Press the paper down gently.

Open the paper and see what you've made.

HAVE FUN WITH BLOTS!

You can touch up the blots to make the picture clearer.

It's very easy to make pictures out of blots . . .

. . . just use your imagination!

an insect

a horse's head

a flower

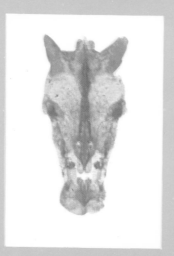

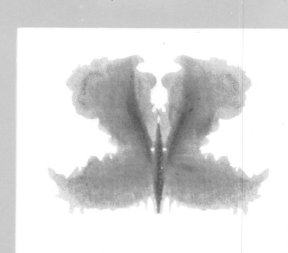

A LITTLE INK.......
A LOT OF BLOW

Ink,
a sheet of paper,
a dropper,
a straw.

THE TREE

Use the dropper to put **a large drop of ink** (or very thin paint) at the bottom of the paper. Holding the sheet of paper at chin level, blow on the ink drop **through the straw.** The straw shouldn't touch the ink. The ink should be blown upwards to make a shape on the paper. Add another drop and blow in different directions to form the branches.

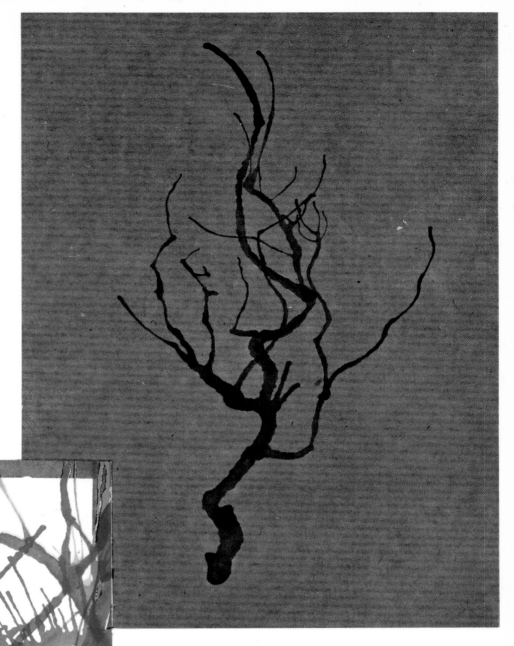

UNDERWATER SEASCAPE

Use different-colored inks (or paints thinned well with water).

Let each color dry before you use another.

Cut out some fish and glue them on.

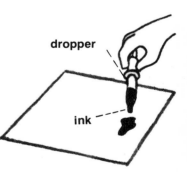

dropper

ink

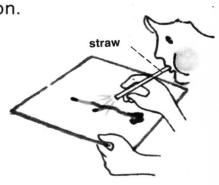

straw

BUTTERFLIES

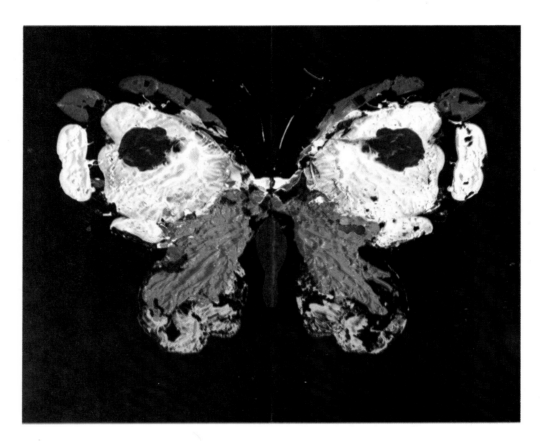

Using thick paint (straight out of a tube or very thick poster paint) put some splotches on a sheet of paper, following the pattern of the first sketch below.

Fold the paper in two.

Press down very gently.

Open it up . . .

some splotches . . .

fold in half . . .

press gently . . .

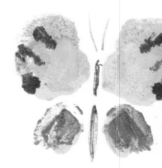

open up.

A BOUQUET OF FLOWERS

Take **a paper doily.**

Cut out a smaller circle of **plain paper** and glue it in the center.

Now make the bouquet: Using paint or felt pens make lots of different colored splotches on the paper; these are the flowers (1).

With black ink or a black felt pen, give each flower a center (2).

Add the finishing touches with some flowers and petals drawn in black (3).

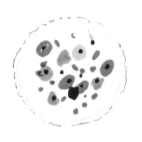

1   2   3

FINGER PRINTING

Use fairly thick paint (poster paint will do).
Dip your index finger in it. Use your finger to make light and dark imprints on the paper (see sketch below).

Make **flowers** with a dark fingerprint for the center and five colored fingerprints around it for the petals.

Make **butterflies** with fingerprints for wings. A large and a small fingerprint on each side of the body make a butterfly (above).
For the butterfly in flight (below) make only two overlapping fingerprints.

THE LEOPARD

Trace the outline of a leopard on to yellow paper and cut it out. Give him a stripe down his back by shading gently with an orange pencil.

Use your index finger, dipped in black paint, to make his spots. By using more or less paint and by pressing down more or less heavily, you can make his spots lighter and darker. It is best to put bigger spots down the center and smaller ones at the sides.

A TREE IN AUTUMN

Secure a sheet of paper firmly in place with pins.
Draw or paint a tree trunk and a few branches.

To make the leaves:
Prepare some fairly thick yellow and red poster paint.
Dip one finger from one hand into the yellow paint and one finger from the other into the red paint. (You can use more than two fingers if you like.) Pass your fingers lightly up and down over the paper to make the leaves. (Imagine you are playing a piano — but very lightly!)

Try using your fingers in this way to make a branch of spring blossoms in delicate, pale colors.

FRUITS

Draw the outline in pencil.
Use thick poster paint.
Dip your fingertips in the paint and make little fingerprints of color all over the surface of the fruit. Make the fingerprints overlap for an effect of light and dark.

For a cleaner outline, use a stencil. (See how to make a stencil on the next page.)

STENCILS

1

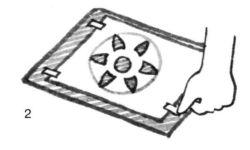

2

On stiff paper, draw **a simple design** — taking care that you leave a space between each part of the pattern.

Cut out the parts that you are going to paint with sharp scissors or a special knife (a cutter) (1).

Put the stencil securely over a sheet of paper (2).

Prepare some thick **poster paint** in different colors.

The best kind of brush to use is a special **stencil brush,** shown above. Paint inside the stencil to make the pattern that you drew (3).

Leave to dry.

Take off the stencil and keep it to use again.

Before using a different color, always wash your brush and let it dry.

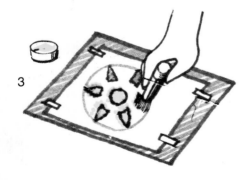

3

A brush with very short, hard bristles can be used instead of a stencil brush.

HORSES

When you make a stencil, the shape that you cut away can be used as shown on the left.
Fix it on to a sheet of paper with straight pins.
Paint around the shape.
Take off the shape.

Trace the outline of a horse on to a piece of cardboard and cut out the shape.

Tape the stencil firmly on to a long piece of paper (try using brown paper).

Fill in the first horse, using black paint.

Leave to dry.

Use the stencil to make more horses, overlapping each other. Use less paint for the ones in the background to make them lighter, as if they were further away.

Use the same stencil for all the horses.

GOUACHE

Thin the gouache with a little water to make a **thick, creamy paint.**

Use good brushes with soft bristles in all sorts of thicknesses for varied effects.

To cover large surfaces well, use a large brush and plenty of paint. Gouache properly prepared **covers** well.

Use your paints and brushes to make . . .

A HARLEQUIN

Have fun making this harlequin's costume, using all the colors you have and mixing lots of new ones.

See the effect when . . .

You paint on thick, colored paper.

Use lighter and darker shades of the same color. Mix white paint with a color — the more white you use, the lighter it becomes (see the hen's tail).

**For best results,
draw an outline of your picture first.**

A ROLLER....

Prepare the gouache:

In a saucer, thin some gouache with a drop or so of water to make quite a large amount of **thick, smooth paint** (1).

Roll the roller in this until it is well covered (2).

BOATS AT SEA

The sky: Make a blue background by passing the roller back and forth across the page (3). Start at the top and make the bands of color overlap so that there are no gaps. Leave to dry.

The sea: With a pencil, lightly draw in three wavy lines.
By adding different amounts of white paint to green paint, produce three different shades of green.

With the roller and light green paint, make a band, following the highest wavy line.
With the mid-green shade, make a band following the second wavy line.
With the dark green, make a band of color at the foot of the page, following the last wavy line.

The sails: Cut out, color and stick down triangles of paper. The largest sails go furthest down the page.

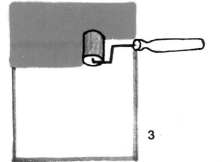
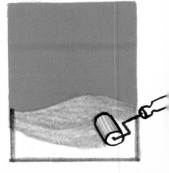

1   2   3

....AND GOUACHE

THE CITY

Use colored paper if you have it.

The sky is made with a roller of paint that is almost dry. With a small roller and different colors of paint, make bands of color from the bottom of the page up the paper — the buildings.

Wash the roller well and leave to dry before changing colors. Add a few strokes for the windows, with a brush.

ROLLERAMA

Make lots of mysterious patterns. The shapes vary according to how much paint you use and how thick it is. Roll the roller up the paper, across the paper or in wavy lines and experiment for the best effects. Use different colors on top of each other for exciting patterns.

Use the patterns you have created to decorate record covers, greeting cards, book jackets and book-marks.

The lightness of water and
the clarity of color together make

WATER-COLOR

Wet a sheet of **thick paper** thoroughly with a piece of cotton soaked in water.

Take some **very runny water color** and a very soft brush.

With the point of your brush, touch the paper gently.

See how the color **spreads** over the paper.

Use more colors and watch the effects.

LANDSCAPE

Make a very light drawing.

Wet the paper with cotton or a brush and water. Very gently paint in the sky and the ground . . . running different colors into one another and not paying too much attention to detail. Any details you wish to put in are added later when the paper is dry.

THE LITTLE GIRL

Make a fine pencil drawing. Wet the hair, and immediately add a drop or so of very runny orange and brown paint. Wet the bouquet and allow a few drops of color to merge together.

Colored inks can be used instead of water color.

PEACH BLOSSOM

Make a very fine drawing.

Paint the branch with clear water.

Touch the branch with water color —
this should spread down the whole
branch.

Add some more color if necessary.

For the flowers: wet each petal
separately and add a drop of color,
always from the center of the flower out-
wards.

Leave to dry and then add the flower
centers with dots of color.

THE LEAF

Wet the shape you have drawn.
Add a few drops of color. Leave to dry.
The colors will form a pattern of their
own.

Wet and paint each part of a drawing separately.

PORTRAIT

BUTTERFLY

THE INVISIBLE OUTLINE

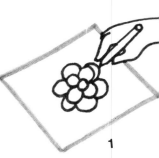

1

2

Make a very light pencil drawing of the flower (1).

Follow the outline of the petals with glue (using the nozzle of the tube just like a pencil). Try to have as few breaks as possible (2).

Leave to dry well.

With a soft brush and paint or colored ink, paint over the whole flower, the color slides over the glue, **leaving the outline clearly visible.**

Paint around the flower with dark paint or India ink.

3

THE HOUSE

Make a light drawing of a house.
Draw over the outline with glue.
Leave to dry thoroughly.
Cover with blue ink.

BIRD

Make a light drawing of a bird.

Draw over the outline with rubber solution (this is a kind of glue). Leave to dry.

Paint with **different colored inks.** Leave to dry again.

If you go over the whole picture gently with an eraser, the rubber solution disappears and you are left with a white outline.

FISH

In this picture, draw over the outline with the edge of a candle.

Draw over the outline of the waves with glue.

Draw over the outline of the plant with a wax crayon.

Paint the picture when the glue is dry.

ABSTRACT PAINTING

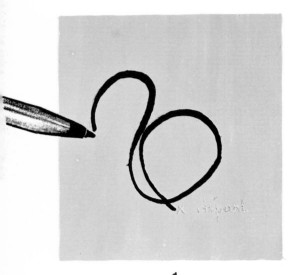

1

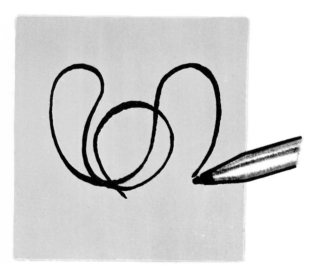

2

3

With your eyes almost shut, draw a shape with a pencil or felt pen on a piece of paper (1).

Carry the line on to make pleasing shapes (2).

Spread over all the paper and join up any loose ends (3).

Paint (with gouache, colored inks or felt pens).

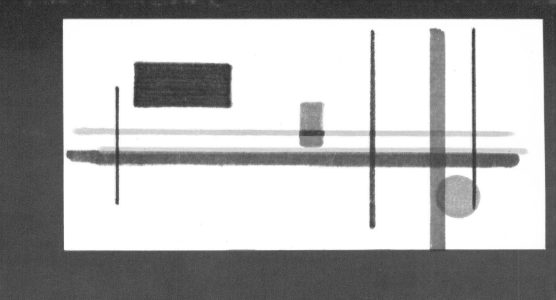

PAINT PATTERNS

Above: With or without a ruler, draw lines across and up and down the page. Add patches of color in different shapes.

Below: Draw a long line down the page. Draw a pattern down it as shown (a, b, c).
Paint in the shapes you have made.

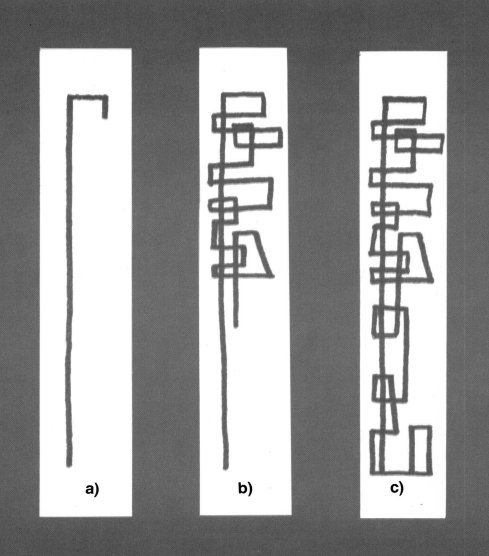

a)

b)

c)

FLOATING COLOR

1

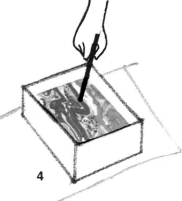

2

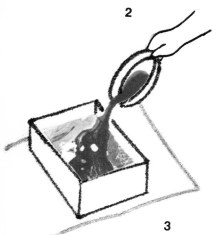

3

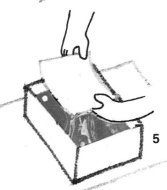

4

You need:
Old newspapers,
a tank or some water tight container
    three-quarters full of water,
oil paints in different colors,
oil,
a stick,
white or colored sheets of paper.

On the newspaper, place the container three-quarters full of water (1).
If the paint is too thick, thin it with a little oil to make a thick cream (2).
Pour a little paint into the water (use different colors) (3).
Stir very gently with the stick (4).
Put a sheet of paper on the surface of the water (5).
Take it off carefully. It should have a pattern of paint on it (6).
Leave it on an old newspaper to dry thoroughly.

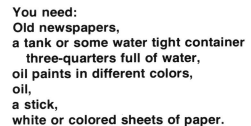

5

Black paint and one drop of green paint on red paper.

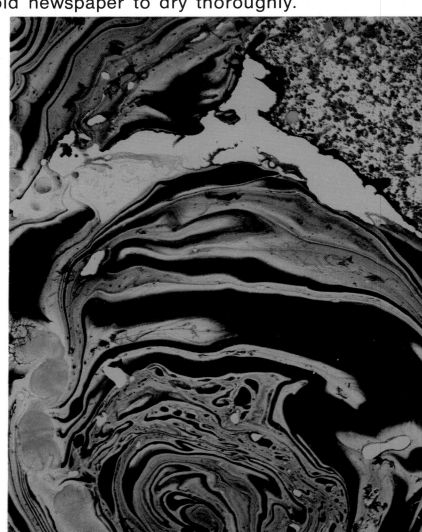

When you have finished, clean out your container with a rag and turpentine — but do this well away from any fires.

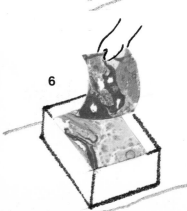

6

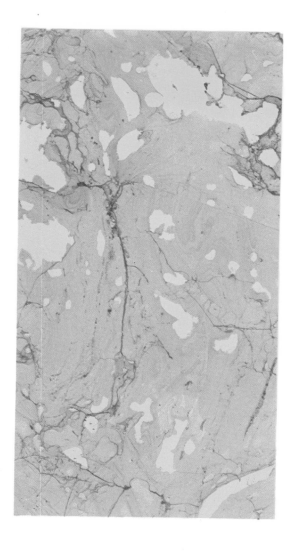

Yellow paper and blue paint.

With this very simple method — and a lot of care — you will be able to achieve fantastic effects. You will be surprised at their endless variety and the extreme delicacy of their outlines.

You can easily make:

MARBLE GALAXIES

SEASCAPES

PRECIOUS STONES...

The results will vary according to how much paint you use and the color of your paper.

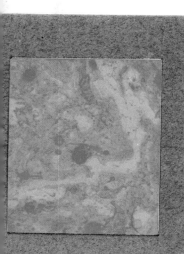

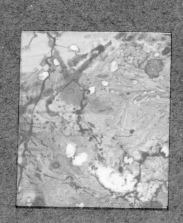

OIL PAINTING

Is it really so difficult? Not at all!
And remember, unlike water color and poster paints, you can paint over your mistakes.
Clean your brushes with turpentine. This is also used for thinning down oil paints.
Preferably, you should paint on canvas or specially coated paper.

THE CLOWN

1. Make a rough drawing in pencil (or charcoal).
2. With your brushes, build up the colors stroke by stroke, starting with the face.
3. Finish the background.
   The whole surface should be covered.

FISHING BOATS

1. Start by covering the whole surface with a gray-green background.
    On a palette mix a little of each of the following:

    **Naples yellow
    Cobalt blue
    Umber
    and a lot of white.**

    With a large brush and the color you have just mixed, paint across the background starting at the top. These streaks of color form the ground.

2. Draw the boats with pencil and outline them with dark paint — a mixture of cobalt blue and umber.

3. Add some strokes of light color to the sides of the boats. Finish by painting in the shadows of the boats.

FIREWORKS

Secure a sheet of paper in place with pins.
Press hard on to a tube of paint, holding it down on to
the paper. Then drag the tube out from the center, sending
sparks of paint in all directions.

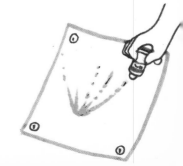

By reading this book and following its simple instructions, you have learned to paint with gouache, like this

with water color, like this

with oil paints, like this

with many other ways to find out that it's Lots of Fun to Paint.

And now . . . paint ME if you can!